1   Fill in the missing letters to
make words that rhyme.

bark

_ _ ark

rain

_ _ ain

pair

_ _ air

2

Match the kittens into pairs.
Which kitten is on its own?

😊 A fun way to learn the concept of pairs.

3 Count the jewels. Are there more on Princess Natalie's dress or her cloak?

4

Which pirate is known as Smelly Jim?
Use the clues to work it out.

He has a patch on his eye.

His t-shirt has stripes.

He has bare feet.

😊 Gain reading confidence by solving the clues.

5   **Match up the pairs of items
in this messy bedroom.**

☺ **Have fun learning the concept of pairs.**

Find the correct end to each word
and draw lines to join them together.

hippo

kanga

rhino

croc

roo

ceros

odile

potamus

☺ Begin to tackle some long but familiar words.

7 Draw more matching shapes on the scarves
so there are 10 shapes on each.

Choose the correct spelling for each item.

draggon
dragin
dragon

wizard
wizid
wizad

furry
farey
fairy

 Learn how to spell some fairy story words.

9 Complete the alphabet on the magic carpet.

☺ Practise forming letters neatly.

Which two of these pictures are exactly the same?

a

b

c

d

e

f

☺ Look closely and develop observation skills.

Read the story and colour the picture to match.

The little blonde fairy did a twirl. 'Do you like my new blue dress?' she asked Pink Rabbit. 'It matches my tail,' said Rabbit. 'And my purple ears are the colour of that toadstool!'

Make up more stories using colour words and description.

True or false? Circle the correct answer each time.

The boat is on the water. True? False?

The boat is on the land. True? False?

The cat is on the boat. True? False?

The cat is on the land. True? False?

 Investigate the difference between true and false.

13 Which part of the monster's face is covered in each picture? Copy the words into the correct arrow.

nose   ears   eyes

 Practise writing simple, useful words.

14

Say the words out loud and listen to the start sounds.

15

Which of these comical spiders was drawn by Richie?

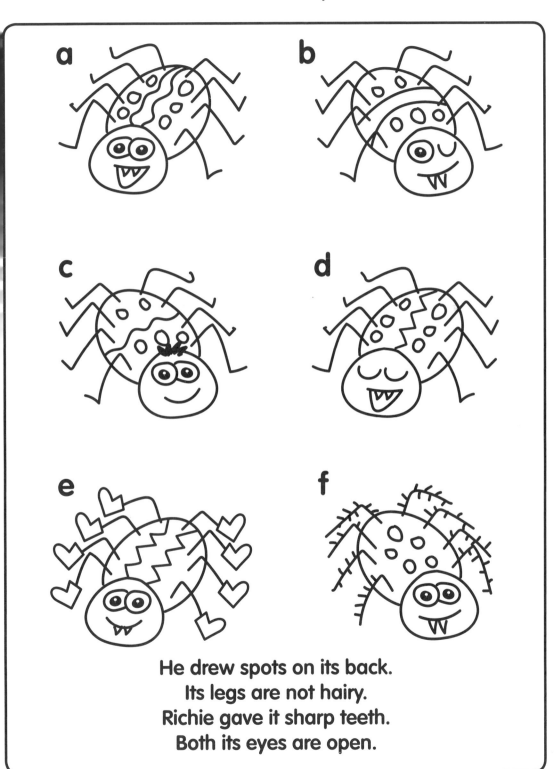

He drew spots on its back.
Its legs are not hairy.
Richie gave it sharp teeth.
Both its eyes are open.

🙂 Tune in to the logical side of the brain.

Draw a circle around the word that goes with each picture.

dip dig did

pin pan pen

jar far bar

 Investigate different word sounds.

17 Which numbers are missing from the phone? Write them in the correct order.

18 Which word describes the way each creature moves? Write in the spaces.

swim   run   hop   fly

19

Can you find 6 fairy wands hidden in the picture?

🙂 **Look for items that are out of place.**

Draw arrows to match each word to the correct picture.

high
low

clean
dirty

full
empty

😊 **Recognise that describing words can have opposites.**

21 Look for each of the colour words hidden in the grid.

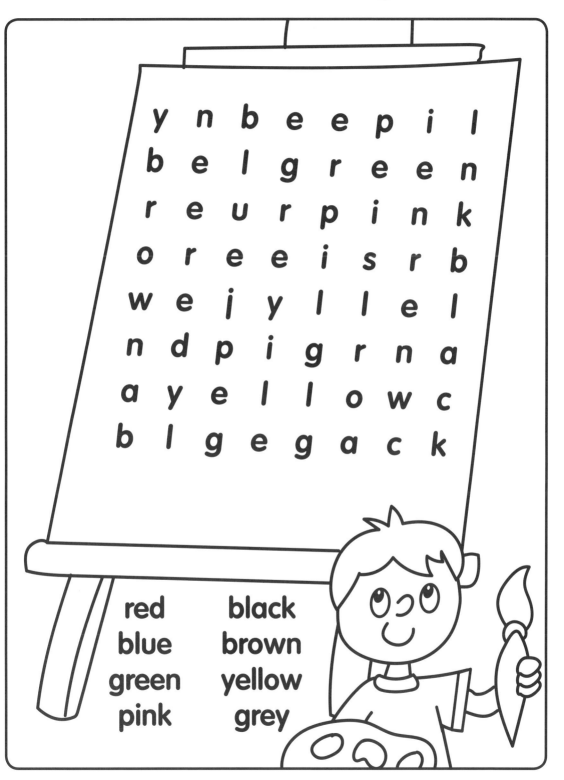

y n b e e p i l
b e l g r e e n
r e u r p i n k
o r e e i s r b
w e j y l l e l
n d p i g r n a
a y e l l o w c
b l g e g a c k

red   black
blue   brown
green   yellow
pink   grey

☺ Increase familiarity with common, useful words.

22

Colour in the coins you need to buy a spinner.

55

75

20

35

10 10 10 10 5

10 10 10 5 5

😊 Learn to use coins as they are used in real life.

Unscramble the sets of letters to spell the monster body parts.

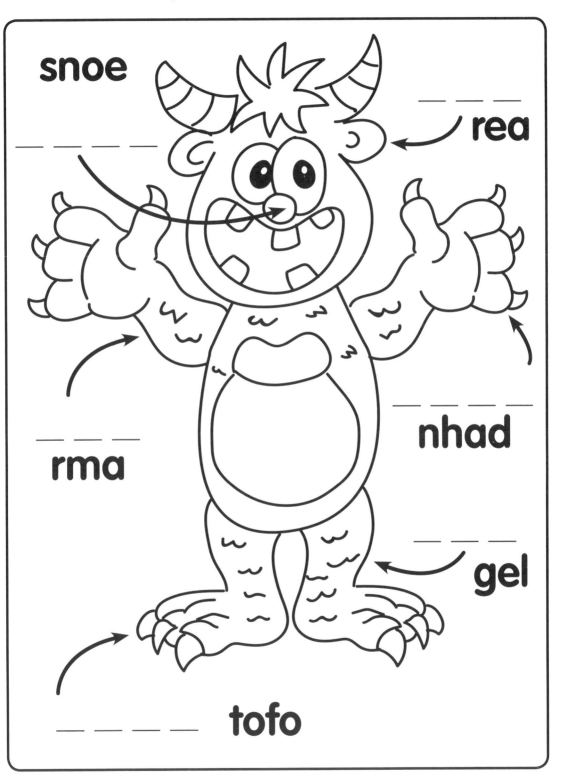

snoe

rea

rma

nhad

gel

tofo

Practise spelling using simple anagrams.

Match the snowflakes into identical pairs.

25 Complete the alphabet on the sweets decorating this fairy tale cottage.

Pair up the items so that both of them rhyme.

☺ Have fun listening for matching sounds.

Join the creatures that have the same number of legs as each other.

28 Do the maths and draw your answer as jewels.
The first has been done to show you how.

3 + 3 =

2 + 5 =

6 + 2 =

7 − 3 =

9 − 4 =

😊 Make maths more visual with picture answers.

Circle the correct letter in each group
to finish the words.

fee____   f
          d
          t

____ake   c
          s
          m

____ish   v
          f
          p

pon____   n
          g
          d

☺ Recognise beginning and end sounds of words.

30

**Find a path through the leaves
to pick up the acorns.**

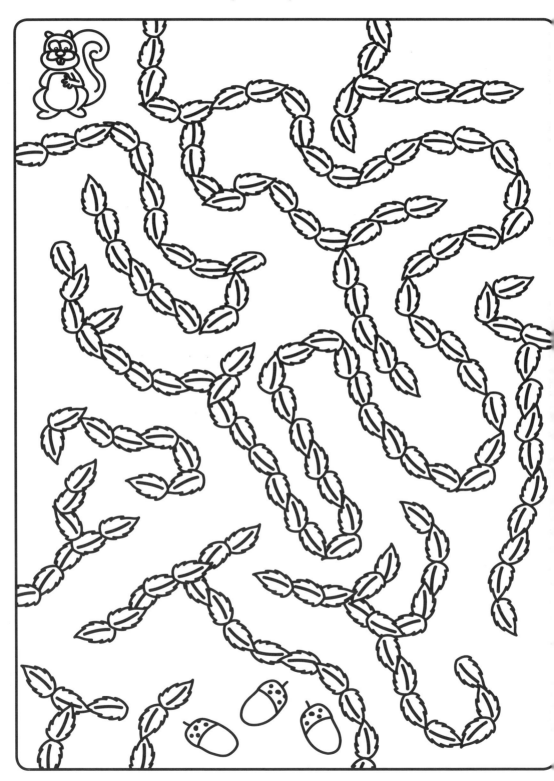

31 What weather is shown in each picture?
Copy the words into the correct space.

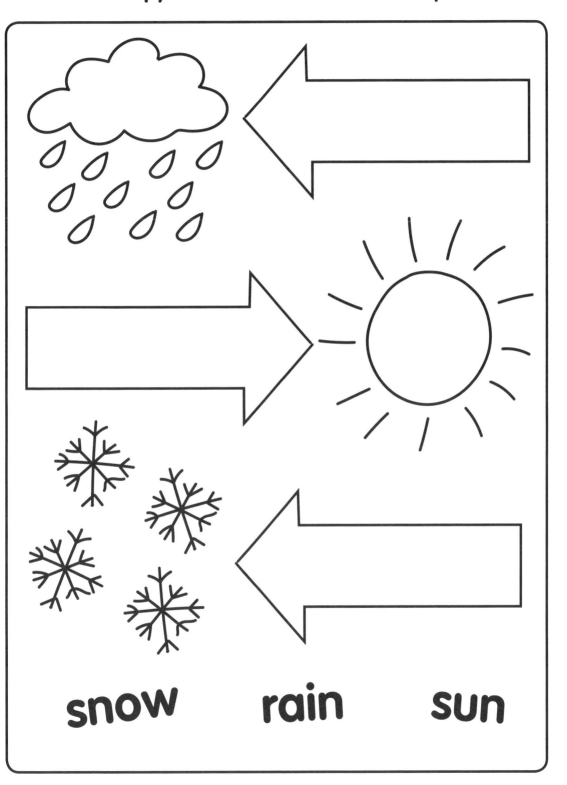

snow   rain   sun

Circle all of the capital letters in this story. Now colour the picture.

Princess Abigail jumped onto her trusty pony, Periwinkle. She had heard that Prince Robert of Ritovia was in trouble. 'Don't worry, I will help you!' she shouted as she reached the Terrible Tower. 'Here I am!'

 Discuss different uses for capital letters.

Circle the rhyming words in
these funny sentences.

The sad girl took
her pet to the vet.

The cub in the
tub needed a
good scrub.

Six boys did tricks with sticks.

 Use rhymes to extend vocabulary.

Match the words to the correct picture each time.

shark

moon

seal

book

cook

shell

😊 **Gain confidence with reading new words.**

35

Look at the two pictures and find six things that are different between them.

Follow the arrows to make your way to the cupcake.

START

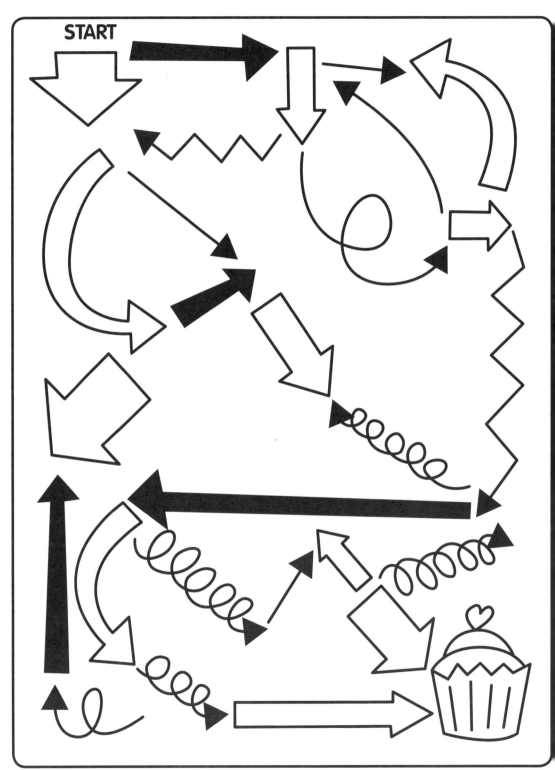

😊 This activity develops progressive thinking and planning.

Colour the owls so there are three of each colour.

☺ Have fun with counting and dividing.

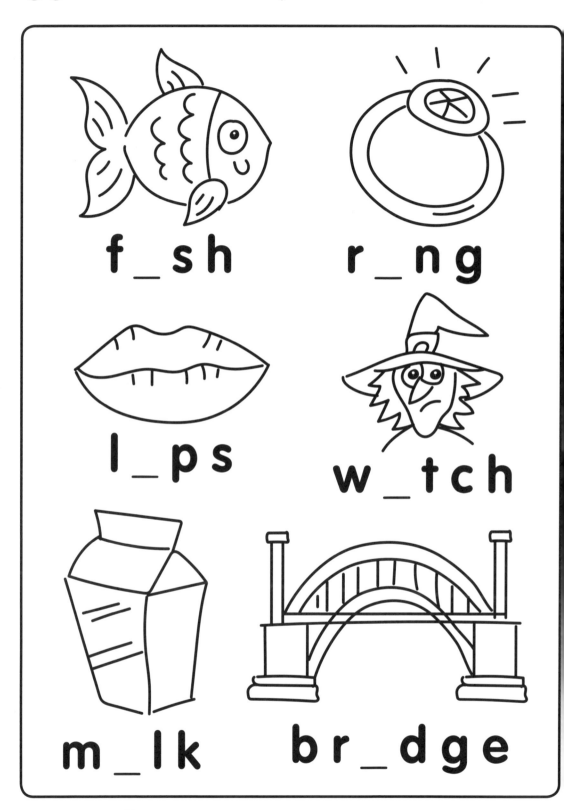

38 Which vowel completes all of these words?

f _ s h

r _ n g

l _ p s

w _ t c h

m _ l k

b r _ d g e

Practise writing simple, useful words.

Fill in the correct word each time.

The plane is _____ the clouds.

The helicopter is _____ the clouds.

The plane looks _____ .

The helicopter looks _____ .

below   old   above   new

☺ **Practise handwriting and opposites in one task!**

Circle the sound that goes at the end of all of these words.

ch   **ck**

th   **sh**

☺ Say the words out loud and identify the end sound.

Which letters of the alphabet are missing here?

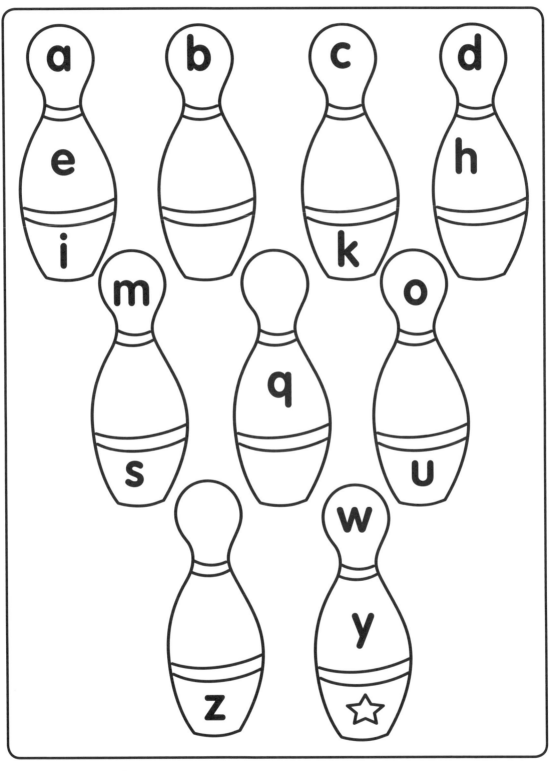

Have fun finishing the alphabet.

Which of these shadow pictures is
an exact match for the main picture?

a

b

c

d

😊 Learn to look very closely and compare items.

43 Colour the words that have the long –a– sound.
What do you notice about the shapes?

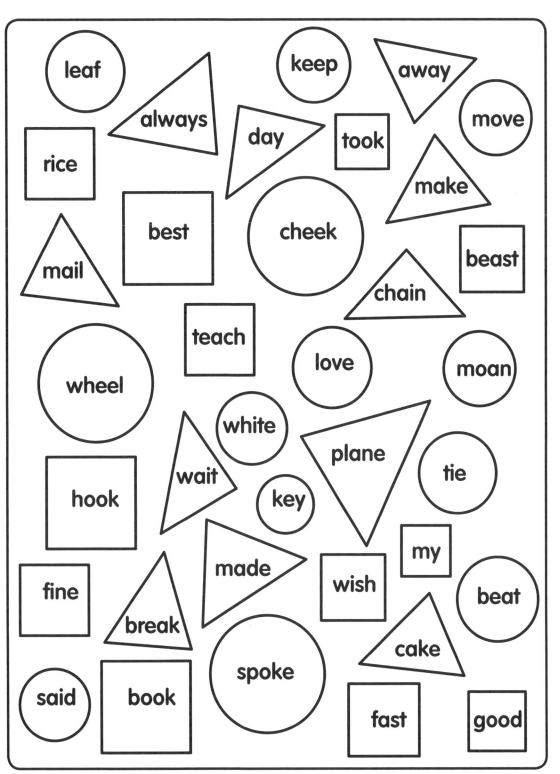

leaf

keep

away

move

always

day

took

rice

make

best

cheek

beast

mail

chain

teach

love

moan

wheel

white

plane

tie

wait

hook

key

my

made

wish

fine

beat

break

cake

said

book

spoke

fast

good

☺ See how different letters make the same sound.

Change the middle sound to make a new word each time.

cat
c _ t

bug
b _ g

man
m _ n

mop
m _ p

Say the words out loud and listen to the differences.

45

Find two diggers that match each other exactly.

a b c d e f g h

Finish writing each of the words, using
the clues to help you.

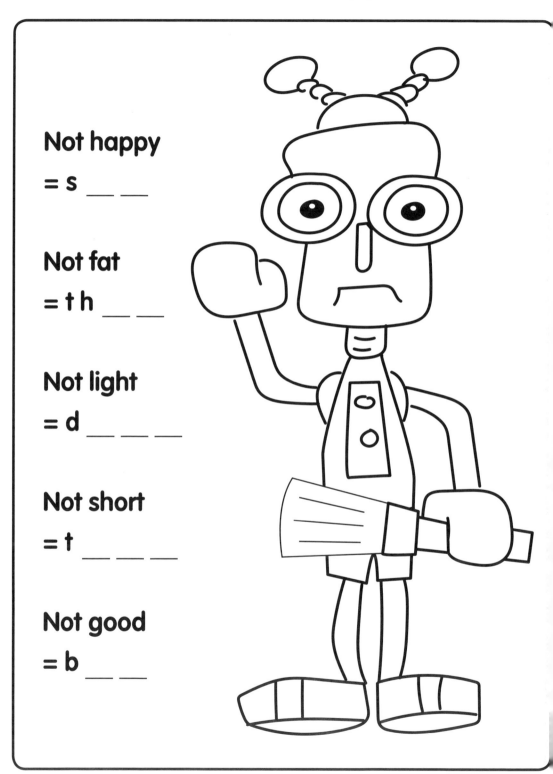

Not happy

= s __ __

Not fat

= t h __ __

Not light

= d __ __ __

Not short

= t __ __ __

Not good

= b __ __

😊 Think about simple opposites and how they are written.

47 Which clock shows the same time as the big clock?

a 12:15

b 2:00

c 4:00

d 2:15

☺ Practise with analogue and digital clocks.

Cross out the word in each group that doesn't rhyme.

face

lace

goose

hand

sad

sand

bell

shell

sheep

Sound out each word to judge which ones rhyme.

49

Which items in the picture begin with the k sound? Remember, they can be spelt with a c, too.

☺ Have fun sounding out words.

50

Finish drawing the patterns on each of the animals.

51 Look for each of the words hidden in the grid.
They are all things that move.

b	l	b	v	a	n	h	p
t	o	o	c	r	s	o	l
p	r	m	a	r	b	o	a
v	r	b	r	y	u	t	n
a	y	a	h	i	s	p	e
s	c	o	o	t	e	r	b
c	b	r	p	b	o	a	t
p	l	b	i	k	e	y	s

car   bike
van   plane
lorry   boat
bus   scooter

52

Join the dots in the correct order to see what is hiding under the waves.

53

**Some of these things do not belong here!
Put a cross next to them.**

54   Find all the circles in this picture. Draw some more balls for the juggler to catch.

🙂 Look for familiar shapes in the real world.

55

Colour the spaces that have a * in them to complete a beautiful night creature.

☺ Have fun with shapes and practise neat pen work.

Match each speech bubble to the correct person.

Get to grips with the world outside home and school.

57 Colour the shapes with four sides and then use the leftover letters to spell a kind of food.

Which of the alien ships is the odd one out?

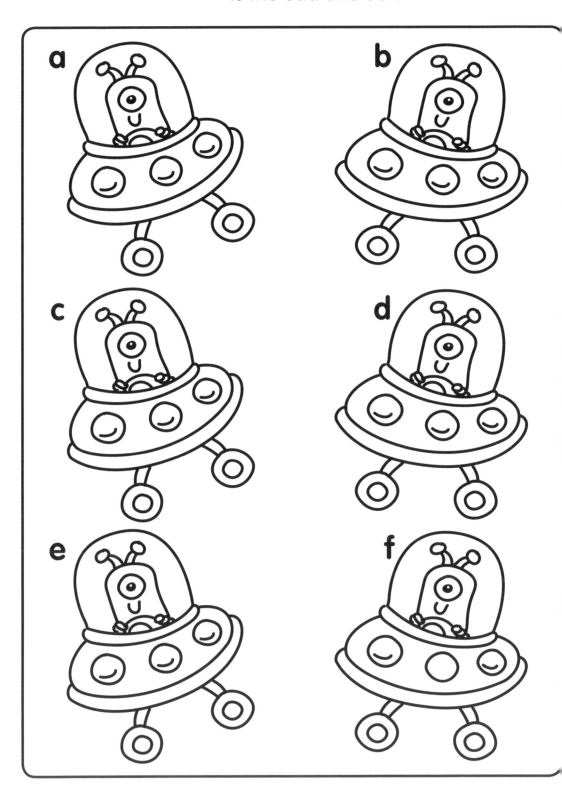

a

b

c

d

e

f

Improve observational and processing skills.

Which of the lines of writing is not a sentence?
Which one is not true?

The dog is in the bath.

The boy is in the bath.

Puddles floor.

The dog is wet.

There is water on the floor.

 Start to understand what a full sentence is made of.

How should you play these instruments?
Copy the correct word next to each picture.

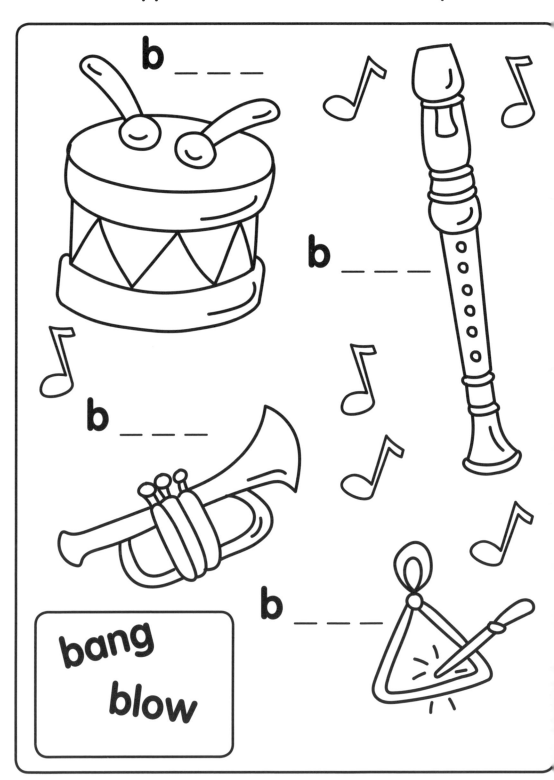

b _ _ _ _

b _ _ _ _

b _ _ _ _

b _ _ _ _

bang
blow

Develop writing skills and knowledge at the same time.

61

Which letter is missing from the start sounds card?

Which shape goes in the empty box?

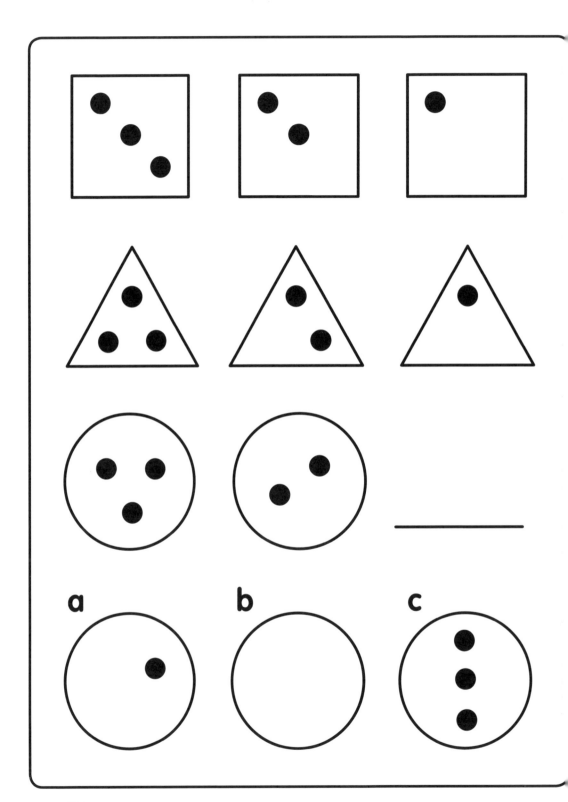

Look for combinations and predict what comes next.

63

Draw lines to match the balls
that have the same numbers on.

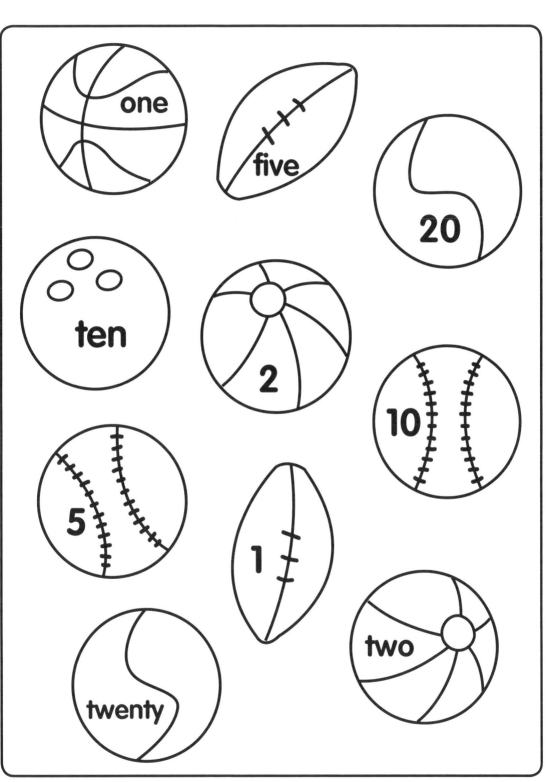

See the links between digits and words.

Sea or sky? Write the words from the list in the correct part of the picture.

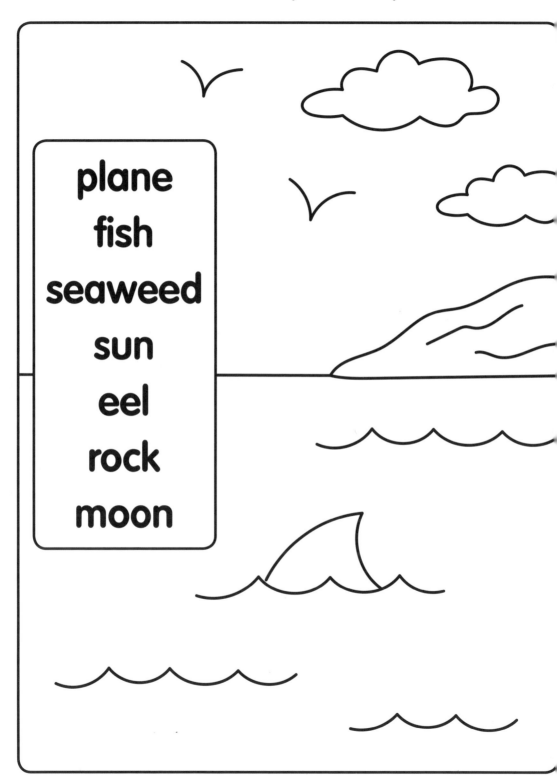

plane
fish
seaweed
sun
eel
rock
moon

Work out where things belong in nature.

65 Make up answers to each of the questions and say them out loud.

What game are they playing?

Who are the two girls?

Where are the girls?

When will they go inside?

☺ Use imagination and learn about question words.

66 Look carefully at the two pictures. Which passengers have got onto the bus in the bottom picture?

😊 A simple but fun exercise in looking at detail.

Draw hands on each clock to show each activity time.

1 o'clock

5 o'clock

68

Each monkey wants three bananas.
Draw rings to share them out.

Fill in the blanks to finish each sentence with your own words.

The zookeeper's name is _____ .

His favourite animal is _____ .

Today he will be cleaning the _____ .

😊 **Have confidence in answering, spelling and writing.**

70

What is missing from these pictures?
Draw them on by yourself.

71

Find a way out of the maze so that the rabbit can eat its carrots.

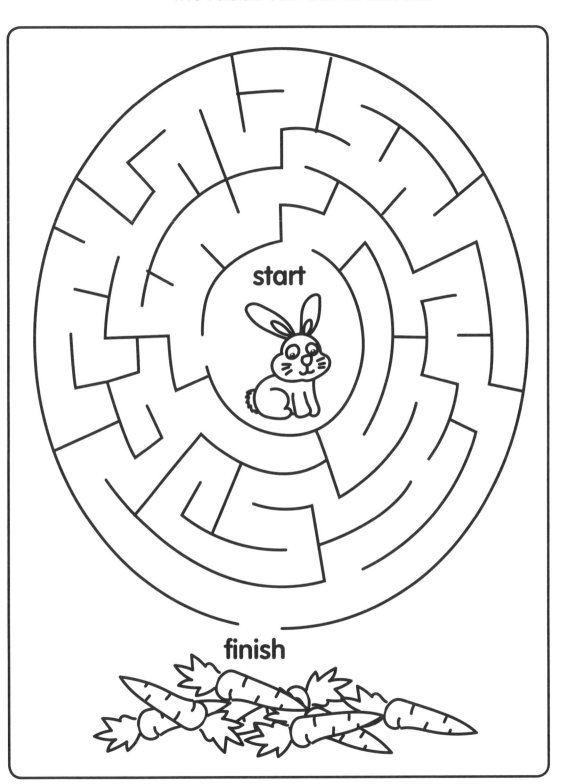

start

finish

Divide the stars into groups of three and colour them different colours.

Make a start on simple division.

What sound does each animal make?
Say them out loud and copy the words.

woof

_____

roar

_____

moo

_____

☺ Enjoy making sounds and writing the letters.

74 Do you know what all these foods are? Say them out loud and circle the sound that starts them all.

d   b   p

Fill in the blanks so the word rhymes
with another word in the sentence.

Cassie learnt
how to bake
a _ _ _ _ .

Jamie needs
some glue for
his _ _ _ _ .

It is too hot
to run in
the _ _ _ .

Build up confidence with words that rhyme.

Put the instructions in the right order, writing the numbers 1 to 4 in the spaces.

☐ Pour on the milk.

☐ Choose a bowl and a spoon.

☐ Put the milk back in the fridge.

☐ Tip cereal into the bowl.

🙂 A comprehension task based on an everyday event.

Finish the dragons so that each one has six spikes on its back.

78 Draw along the dotted lines to match each butterfly to a flower. Colour the pairs with the same colour.

Find a baby dinosaur that looks like each of the big dinosaurs. Draw lines to connect them.

True or false? Circle the correct answer each time.

It is raining outside. True? False?

It is raining inside. True? False?

The fire is lit. True? False?

The curtains are closed. True? False?

🙂 Help your child understand the concept of true and false.

Choose a name from the list that has the same start sound as each animal.

Wendy
Pixie
Zack
Emily
Colin
Max

_____

_____

_____

 Have fun with sounding out names.

Where do the missing pieces fit in the jigsaw?

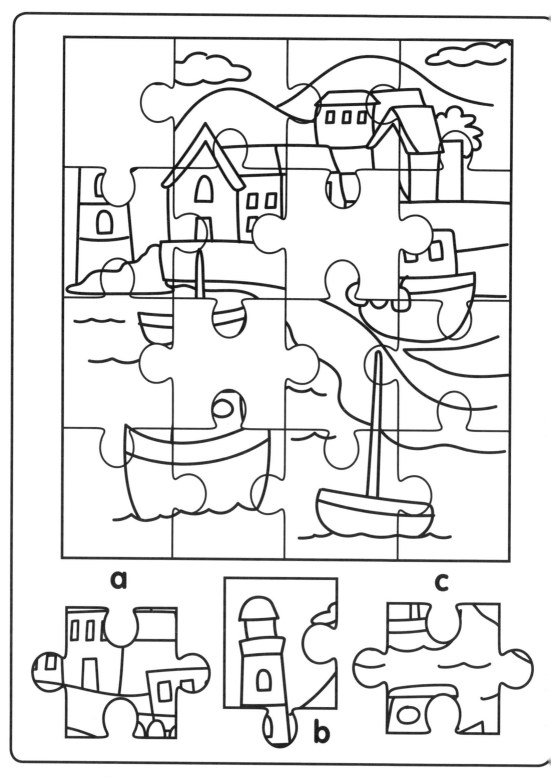

Have fun matching shapes and pictures.

Cross out the word in each group that doesn't rhyme.

😊 Get better at recognising rhyming words.

84

Which tasty snack has the right letters on it to spell cheese correctly?

 Make a start with spelling slightly longer words.

85

Count the footprints to see which monster has taken the most steps.

😊 Counting can be fun and extremely satisfying!

Circle all of the capital letters in this story.

Marty Mouse and his friends Clio and Rufus were best friends. They went everywhere together. On Sunday, they walked to the big city of Merryvale. They were looking for the Ginger Giant!

 Investigate how capital letters are used.

87 Draw two more jewels on each crown.
How many jewels are on each crown now?

Which of the animals is the answer to the riddle?

I have four legs.
I am furry.
I make a great pet.
I have a short, fluffy tail.

 Increase confidence in reading and making decisions.

Fill in the missing letters,
using the clues to help you.

Not here = _ _ _ e r e

Not low = h _ _ _ _

Not inside = _ _ _ _ s i d e

Not dry = w _ _ _

 Work out the opposites of given words.

Which two of these dragons match each other?

How should you play these instruments?
Copy the correct word next to each picture.

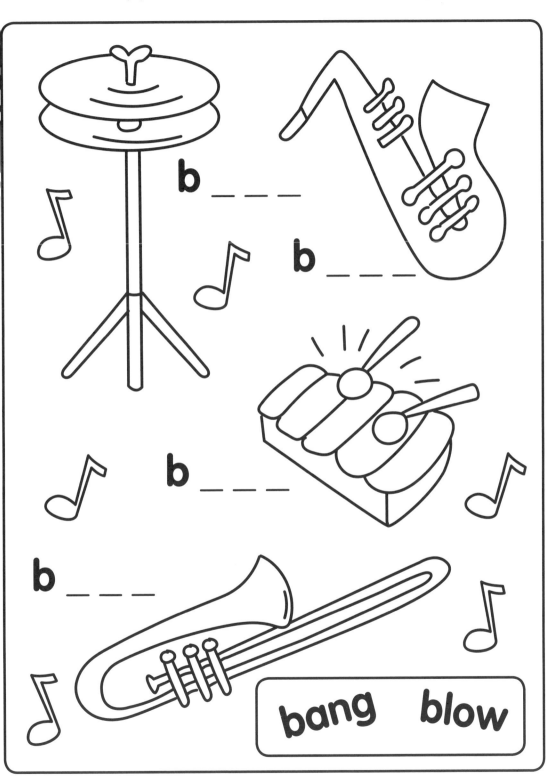

b _ _ _ _

b _ _ _ _

b _ _ _ _

b _ _ _ _

bang   blow

Discuss what you know about musical instruments.

Which shape goes in the empty box?

a   b   c

Look at patterns and predict what comes next.

I spy three words that rhyme with I and spy!
Can you see them?

**Use the number line to
work out the answers.**

Number lines build confidence with adding two numbers.

How tall is the giraffe? Measure it using the blocks that are next to it and circle the right answer.

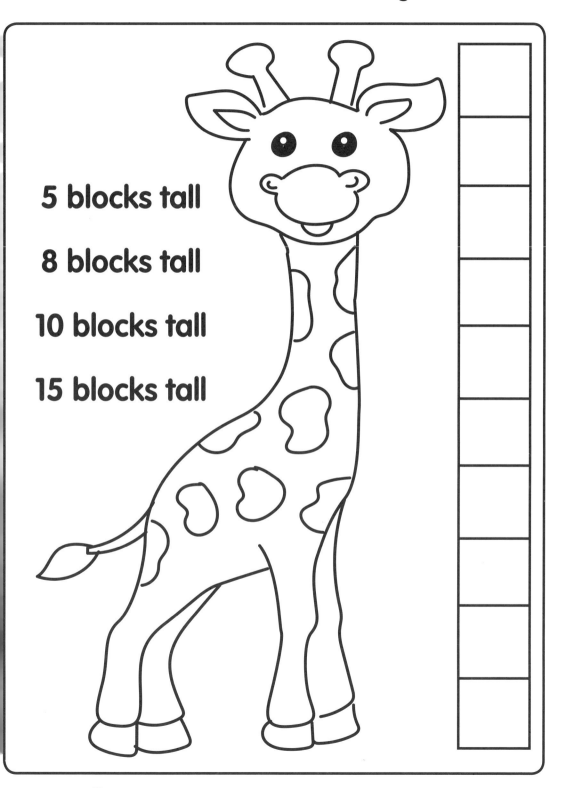

5 blocks tall

8 blocks tall

10 blocks tall

15 blocks tall

Make a start with simple measuring skills.

Draw a circle around the word that goes with each picture.

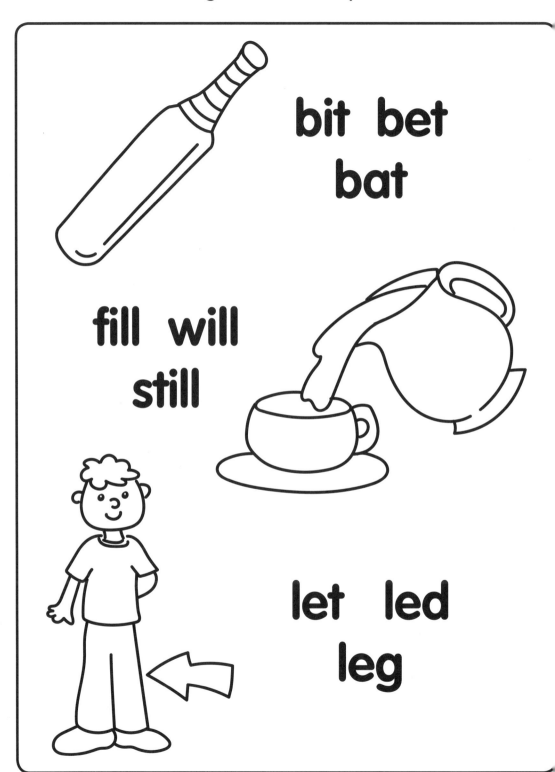

bit bet
bat

fill will
still

let led
leg

 Listen for different word sounds.

Use the number ladder to
help you do the sums.

$2 + 4 =$

$3 + 3 =$

$6 + 2 =$

$5 + 4 =$

$8 + 1 =$

1 2 3 4 5 6 7 8 9 10

😊 Practise addition with a number ladder.

Put the instructions in the right order writing the numbers 1 to 4 in the spaces.

HOW TO PUT AWAY A TENT

☐ Put the tent in its bag.

☐ Take out the tent poles.

☐ Empty your things from inside.

☐ Fold the tent neatly.

Think things through to work in logical steps.

99 Find a path through the grid, connecting the rhyming words. You can move down or sideways each time.

pan	START cat	bag	sad
flag	bat	mat	crab
dad	jam	rat	pan
flag	hat	flat	van
sad	FINISH bat	crab	flag

Read out the first word and then find all the rhymes.

Write the numbers, with 1 on the smallest and 8 on the biggest.

☺ A simple task to learn about ascending order.

Look for each of the insect names hidden in the grid.

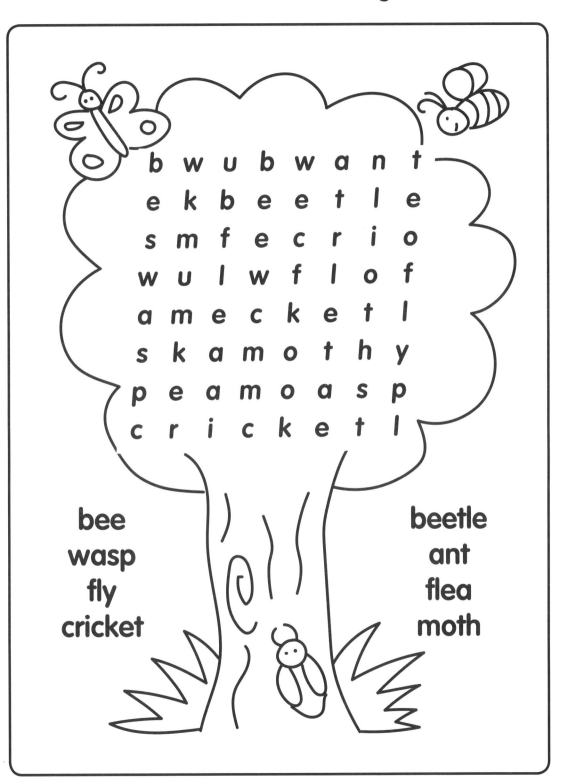

```
b w u b w a n t
e k b e e t l e
s m f e c r i o
w u l w f l o f
a m e c k e t l
s k a m o t h y
p e a m o a s p
c r i c k e t l
```

bee
wasp
fly
cricket

beetle
ant
flea
moth

☺ **Learn to spell everyday words within a category.**

Which whale has the most spots on it?

a

b

c

d

e

f

🙂 Judge numbers by looking as well as counting.

Which of the space rovers is the odd one out?

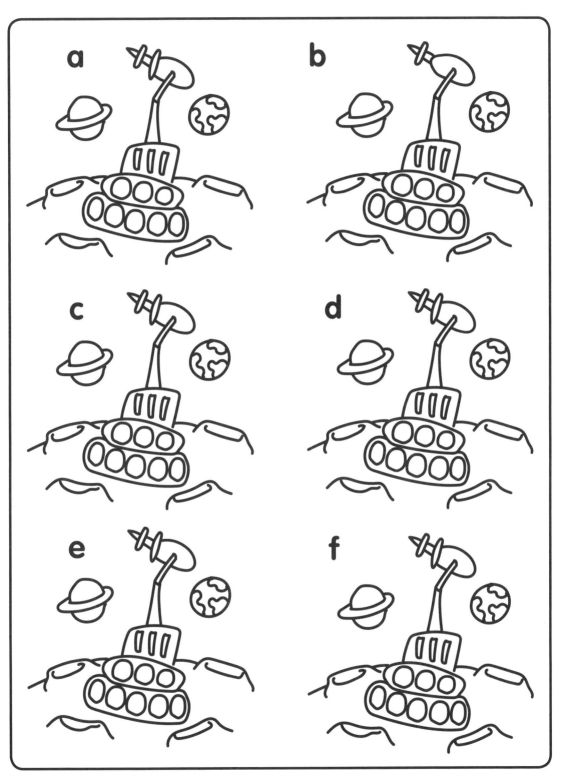

 Develop close observational skills.

Cross out five words that you don't expect to find at the seaside.

sandcastle

reindeer

bucket

radiator

seaweed

spade

crown

toothpaste

rocket

lighthouse

 Read longer words and put them in context.

105

Find two pompoms for each cheerleader
so they add up to 10 for each girl.

These pairs are called number bonds and are useful to learn.

106 Colour the creatures with wings. Use the letters on the other creatures to spell a kind of insect.

Which kite has flown the highest? Add up the numbers on each tail to find out.

🙂 Have fun with simple addition.

What sound does each animal make?
Say them out loud and copy the words.

bear
grrr!

duck
quack!

cat
meow!

Have fun with noises!

Count the items and decide if the answer is odd or even each time.

How many moons on his hat? _____ odd even

How many bolts from his wand? _____ odd even

How many rats by his feet? _____ odd even

How many stars on his gown? _____ odd even

Count and learn about odd versus even numbers.

Can you find six arrows hidden in this scene?

☺ See how quickly specific items are found.

Change a single letter to make each of the new words.

l a k e

**How much money is on
each money plate?**

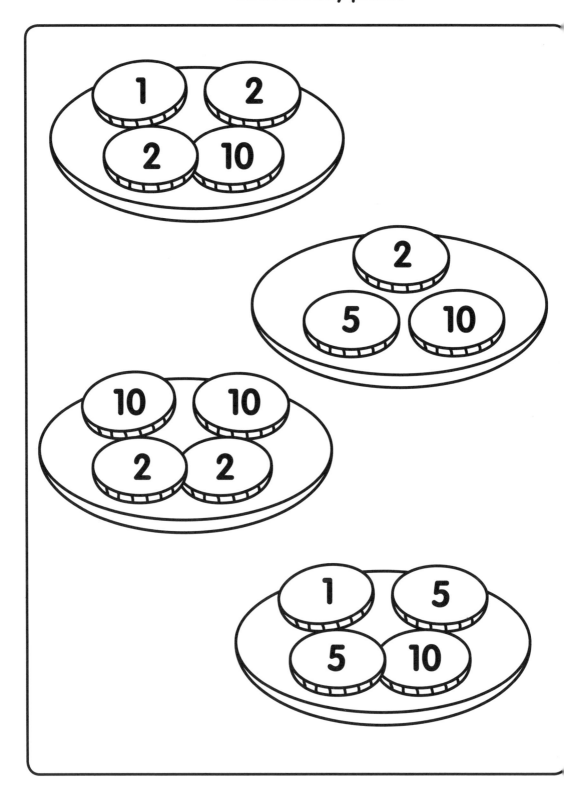

☺ Learn addition using money.

Read the story out loud and then colour the picture to match.

The purple-headed monster gave a loud burp.

His big, red tummy was full of carrots! He loved

carrots because they were orange, like his feet.

His hair was the colour of bananas!

 Have fun with storytelling and description!

114   Copy the words next to the pictures. Where would you be likely to find all these items?

kettle

glass

bowl

fork

milk

eggs

spoon

115 Add an extra letter to each word to make a new word. There are different answers you can choose.

be___

to___   ___it

no___   we___

go___

Verbs are words that describe what you are doing. Draw a ring around the verb in each sentence.

I climb up the ladder.

He lies on the rug.

She buys some apples.

The dog barks loudly.

😊 Learn to identify basic parts of language.

Are these lemons or limes? Colour half of them yellow and half of them green.

118 Which tower is the tallest? Which is the smallest? Draw a new tower that is even smaller.

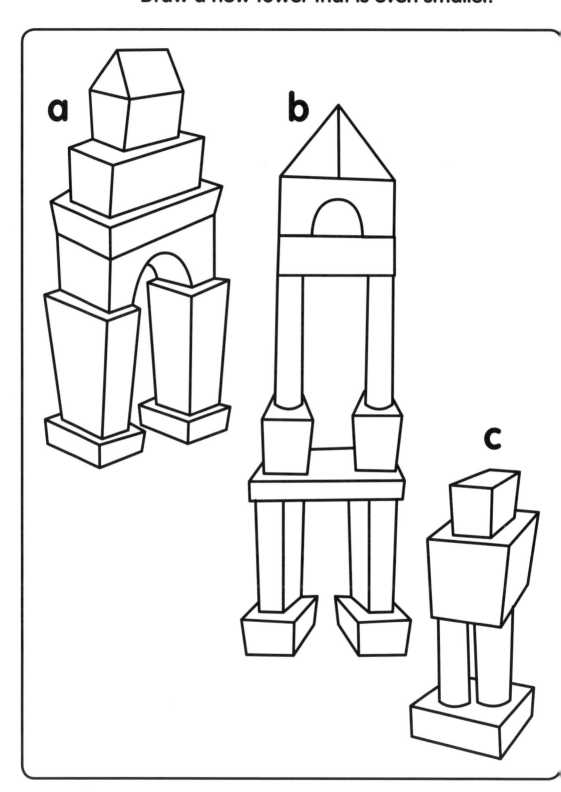

119 Madame Rose is stitching 3 buttons on each sleeve. Work out how many buttons she needs.

120

**Colour each group of fish in a different colour.
Which group has the most fish?**

**Fill in the missing letters,
using the clues to help you.**

Not weak = s t r __ __ __

Not down = __ __

Not old = y __ __ __ __

Not small = b __ __

Think about the opposites of given words.

122

Where do the missing pieces fit in the jigsaw?

123

Fill in the numbers on the wheels, and then use the number line to do the maths.

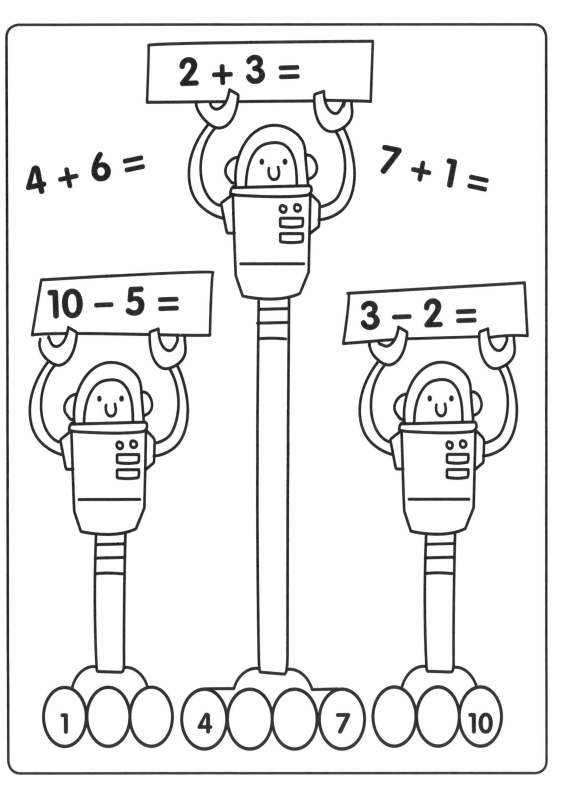

$2 + 3 =$

$4 + 6 =$

$7 + 1 =$

$10 - 5 =$

$3 - 2 =$

1 4 7 10

Using a number line helps with adding and subtracting.

Colour this mermaid however you like, and then fill the gaps with colour words.

The mermaid's tail is _____.

The mermaid's hair is _____.

The fish is _____ and _____.

125

Colour the cars that are facing to the left.
What do the other car letters spell?

Read the complete sentences, and then
fill in the blanks using the correct word.

The boy has six balloons.

The balloons belong to _____ .

These are my presents.

The presents belong to _____ .

😊 Think about different possessive pronouns.

Do the picture sums and write the answer as a number each time.

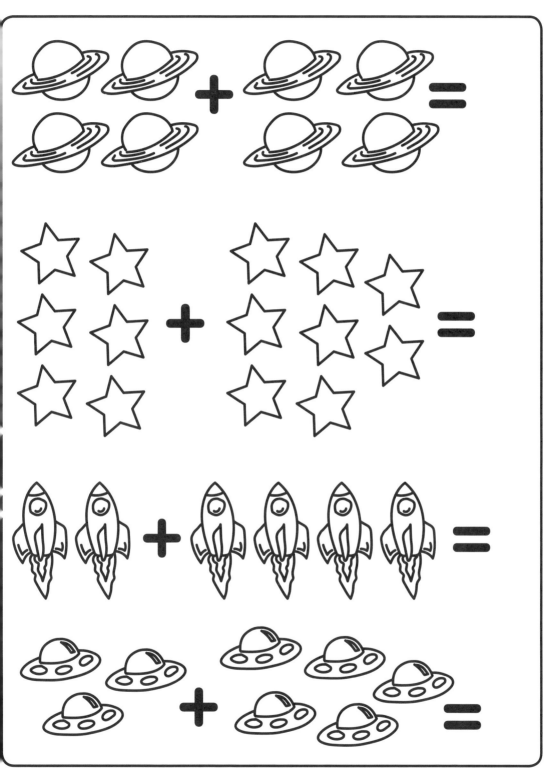

😊 Learn simple addition in a fun way.

Find the sentence that describes something that has already happened.

The sun is shining.

Flowers are growing all around.

The unicorn ate grass for breakfast.

Butterflies flutter overhead.

Investigate tenses with past and present events.

129

**Fill in the missing numbers on the top scarf.
Use it to help you work out the answers below.**

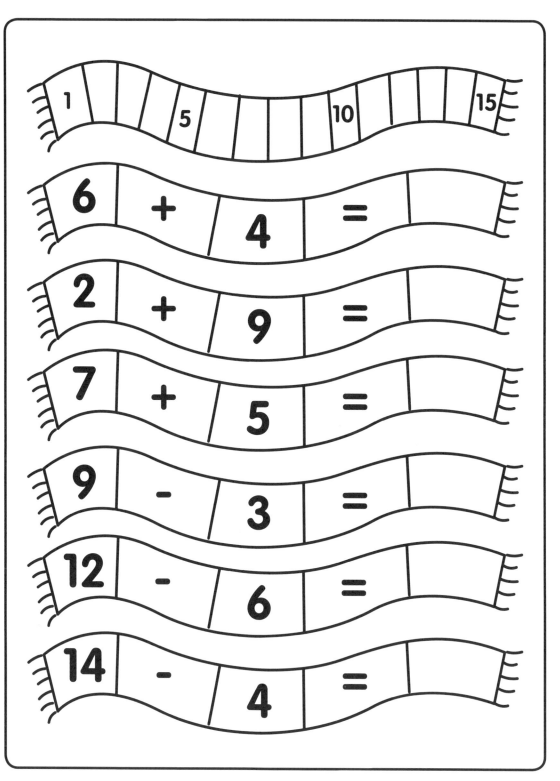

1   5   10   15

6 + 4 =

2 + 9 =

7 + 5 =

9 - 3 =

12 - 6 =

14 - 4 =

☺ **Make your own number line to help with maths.**

130

Colour the balloons with numbers from the ten times table. Remember, they all end with a zero.

20
60
67
50
80
23
49
40

131

Find all of the foods hidden in the grid.

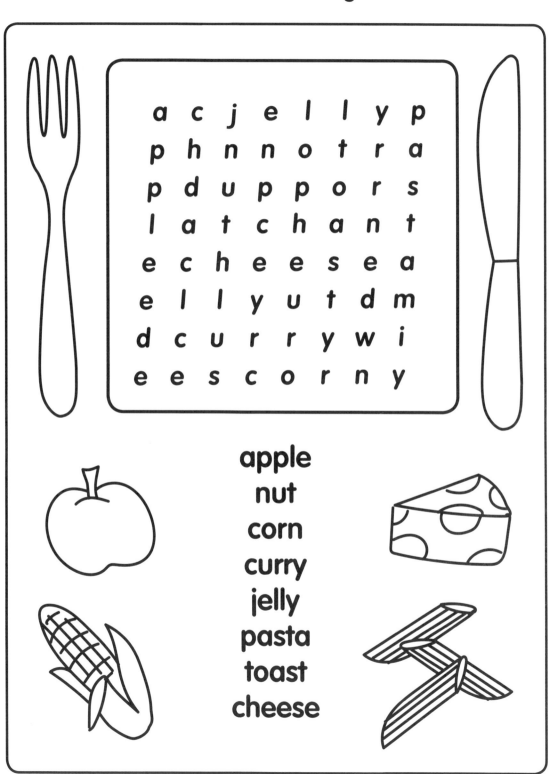

```
a  c  j  e  l  l  y  p
p  h  n  n  o  t  r  a
p  d  u  p  p  o  r  s
l  a  t  c  h  a  n  t
e  c  h  e  e  s  e  a
e  l  l  y  u  t  d  m
d  c  u  r  r  y  w  i
e  e  s  c  o  r  n  y
```

apple
nut
corn
curry
jelly
pasta
toast
cheese

☺ **Learn to spell popular everyday words.**

132

**Which are there more of –
white bats or grey bats?**

**Use the words in the box to
fill in the blank spaces.**

This is E _ _ _ _ . She loves to v _ _ _ _ the

playground. Her Daddy takes her there

after s _ _ _ _ _ sometimes. When she is

feeling brave, she swings h _ _ _ in the air.

Some days, she prefers to swing l _ _ so

her feet can touch the g _ _ _ _ _ .

ground school
Emily low visit high

☺ Practise handwriting and comprehension.

134

Solve the maths problem using the number line at the bottom.

If Goldilocks eats 1 of Daddy Bear's bowls of porridge, 2 of Mummy Bear's bowls, and all 3 of Baby Bear's bowls, how many bowls are left?

1 2 3 4 5 6 7 8 9 10

135

Write the numbers, with 10 on the biggest and 1 on the smallest.

☺ **Introduce the concept of descending order.**

**Which of the sea creatures is the
answer to the riddle?**

I cannot walk on the land.

I swim very fast.

I grow bigger than a person.

I have very sharp teeth!

🙂 **Draw on outside knowledge to help make judgment calls.**

137

Draw hands on the clock to show the times you do these things.

138

Colour this dragon however you like, and then finish the sentences with colour words.

The dragon's wings are _____ .

The dragon's scales are _____ .

The dragon's horns are _____ .

 Tie in creativity with spelling practice.

Add all three numbers on a castle, using the number line to help you.

What sound does each animal make?
Say them out loud and copy the words.

snake
hiss!

sheep
baa!

owl
twit! twoo!

141

Colour half of the vans green and half of them orange. Add the missing wheels, too!

Which of the shooting stars is a little bit different from the others?

😊 Learn to look carefully for small differences.

143

Count the items and decide if the
answer is odd or even each time.

How many jewels on her crown?_____ odd even

How many hearts on her dress? _____ odd even

How many flowers by her feet? _____ odd even

How many butterflies are there? _____ odd even

 Consolidate knowledge about odd and even numbers.

144

Which present matches the one that Jake is holding?

Fill in the missing letters, using the clues to help you.

Not cold = w _ _ _

Not hard = s _ _ _

Not awake = a s _ _ _ _

Not short = l _ _ _

Figure out the opposites of given words.

146

Draw more chicks so that each hen has 5 chicks of her own.

147

**Join the dots in the correct order
to find a magical creature.**

148

Circle the two items that rhyme
in each set of pictures.

149 Number the pods on the big wheel, starting at the very top. Now colour all the odd numbered pods in red.

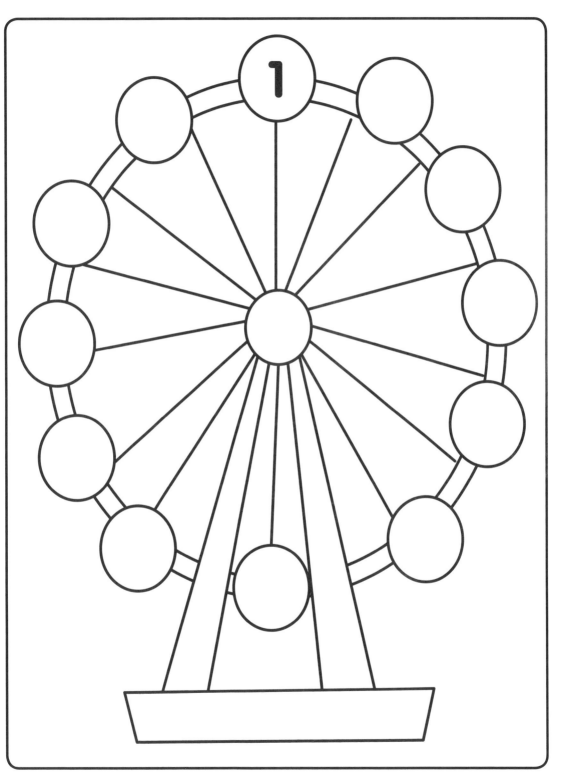

150

Help the clown to get dressed! Put the pictures in order, writing the numbers 1 to 4 in the spaces.

151 Add up the numbers on each tower. Match them to see which tower each knight must climb.

152

Where do the missing pieces fit in the jigsaw?

a

b

c

☺ **Think about how things fit together.**

Draw pictures and write the names for each person on your family tree.

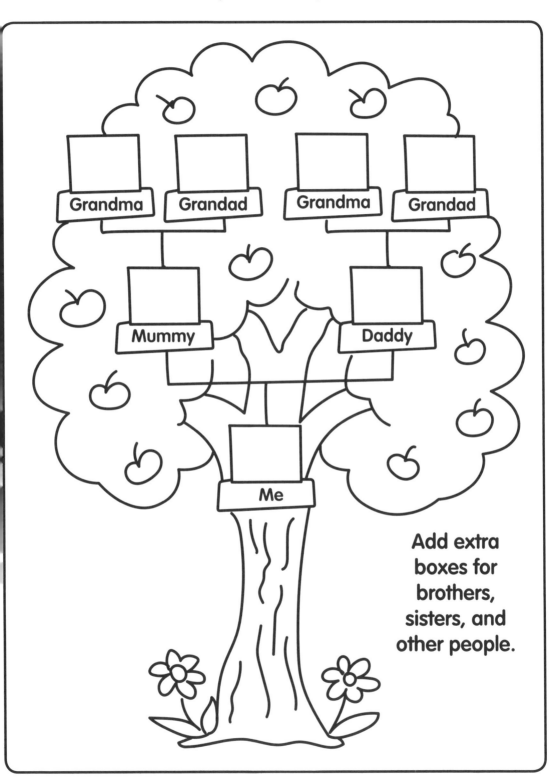

Grandma Grandad Grandma Grandad

Mummy Daddy

Me

Add extra boxes for brothers, sisters, and other people.

🙂 **This helps with handwriting and organising skills.**

154

Can you find Katy's lunch items hidden in the dance studio?

☺ **Pick out and identify hidden items in a scene.**

Read the story out loud and then colour the picture to match.

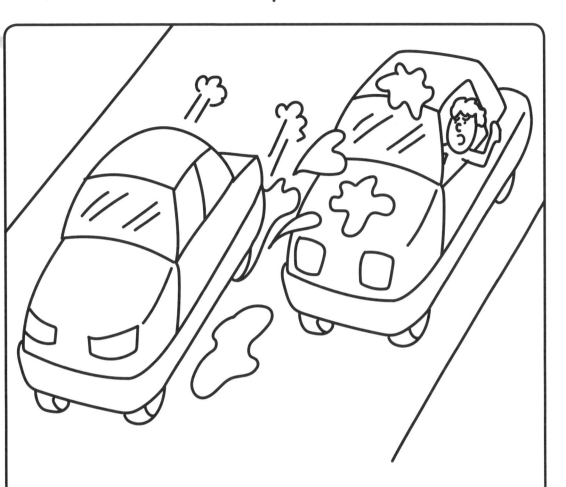

The shiny red car zoomed up behind the bright blue one. 'Watch out for the muddy puddles!' said the driver. 'Too late!' honked the cars, as they were splattered with brown, sticky mud.

 Have fun with descriptions and colouring.

Fill the gaps to complete the blended sound in each item.

h a _ d

f _ a g

t o a s _

p l a n _

😊 Listen for the different sounds in blends.

157

Draw more balloons so that each
elephant is holding three.

:) Have fun with simple maths.

158

**Find two toy robots that match
each other exactly.**

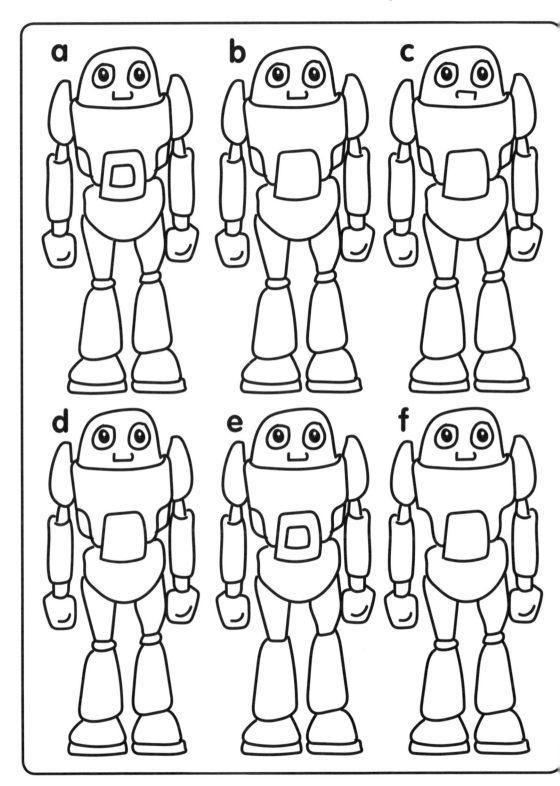

159 Which of the lines of writing is not a sentence?
Which one is not true?

This girl is riding a bike.

The bike has three wheels.

The dog is in front.

Happy dog.

The girl is happy.

 Understand what makes a sentence.

160

Which shape goes in the empty space?

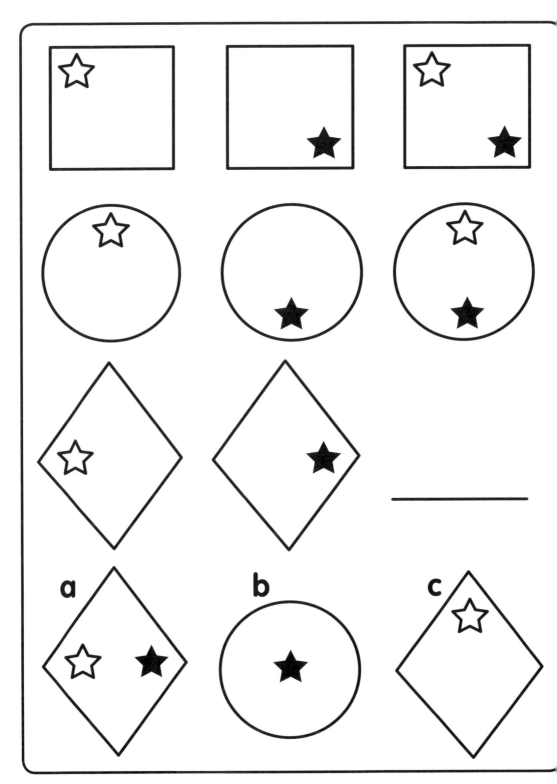

☺ **Find patterns and use them to make predictions.**

Find as many items as you can that begin with the d sound.

😊 **Name lots of items to hear the starting sounds.**

**Which alien has
the most eyes?**

☺ **Judge greater and smaller amounts by sight alone.**

163 How should you play these instruments?
Circle the correct picture next to each one.

164

Draw hands on the clocks to show what time these things take place.

8 o'clock

7 o'clock

165

**Each monster has five lollipops.
Draw rings to share them out.**

Have a go at sharing, or dividing.

166 Find a path through the grid, connecting the rhyming words. You can move down or sideways each time.

**Fill in the footprints,
counting up in tens.**

10 20 30

☺ **Develop number skills in a fun way.**

**Finish drawing the patterns
on each of the items.**

Which letter is missing from the card?
They are all the ending sounds of the words.

See how sounds and letters correspond.

Match the correct speech to each of the people.

Increase knowledge about the world beyond home.

Find each of the words hidden in the grid.
They are all cute and cuddly creatures!

```
s q u i r r e l
w r s g b b o h
h a t g o a t a
a b r r h c i m
n b a l n a y s
d i c a b t a t
o t o m o u s e
g s q b a m b r
```

dog
mouse
cat
rabbit
hamster
squirrel
goat
lamb

☺ Looking for words in a grid helps with spelling.

172

Match the crabs in pairs so that each sum has the correct answer. Use the number line to help you.

4 + 7 =

9 + 3 =

2 + 6 =

5 + 1 =

11

6

8

12

1 2 3 4 5 6 7 8 9 10 11 12

😊 Count with a number line to aid addition.

173 Draw more wheels on the construction vehicles so that each one has four wheels.

 Count on to a given number, and practise drawing circles!

**All of these opposites begin with l.
Can you work out what they are?**

Not early = l _ _ _

Not short = l _ _ _

Not quiet = l _ _ _

Not standing = l y _ _ _

Have fun with opposites.

175 Draw three more craters on each planet.
Count how many there are each time.

176

Cross out the word that doesn't rhyme in each set of pictures.

😊 Link rhyming words and listen for differences, too.

177

Which two clocks show the same time?

a **10:15**

b

c **3:30**

d

e

f **6:10**

😊 Encourage children to read both types of clock face.

**Finish the sentences in
any way you like.**

The fairy's name is _____ .

Her favourite creature is _____ .

When it is sunny, she likes to _____ .

The fairy lives in _____ .

☺ **Expand imaginative thinking and creative writing skills.**

179

How long are the sausage dogs?
Write your answers in the spaces.

This dog is ___ blocks long.

This dog is ___ blocks long.

This dog is ___ blocks long.

Become familiar with measuring items.

180

Colour half of the toadstools red and half of them purple. Add the missing stalks, too!

Fill in the missing words in the story using the list at the bottom.

The little m _ _ _ _ _ couldn't believe it. This was a m _ _ _ _ carpet! Up, up, up into the sky he flew, until he felt that he could touch the m _ _ _ .

moon   **monkey**
magic

 Combine a love of stories with writing practice.

182

**Cross out three creatures each time
and write down your answer.**

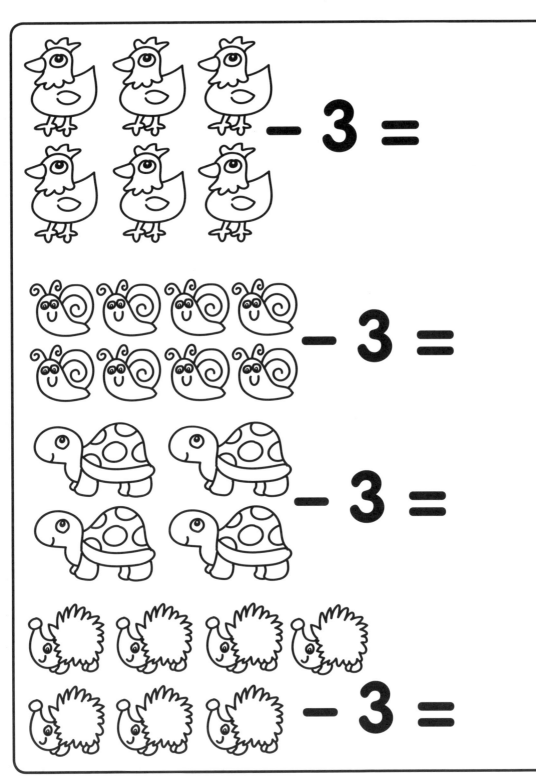

$- \ 3 \ =$

$- \ 3 \ =$

$- \ 3 \ =$

$- \ 3 \ =$

☺ Learn subtraction by crossing things out.

183

Which toadstool has the correct letters to spell magic?

Put spelling skills to the test in a novel way.

Which of these shadow pictures is an exact match for the main picture?

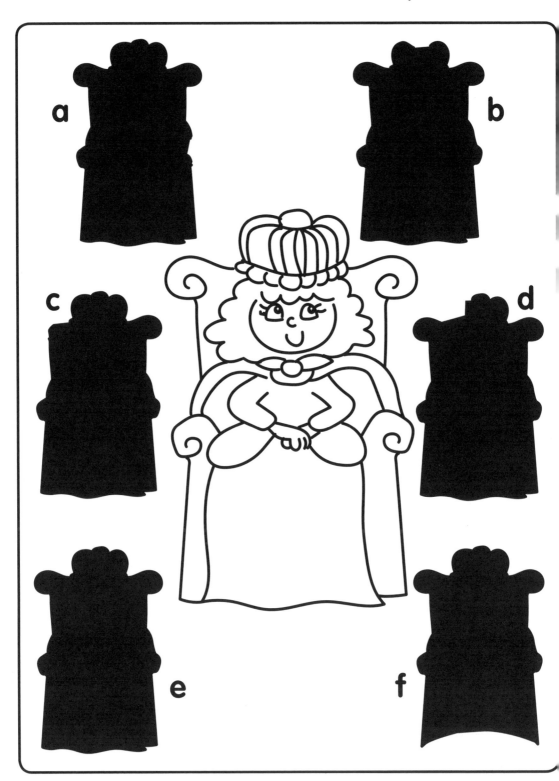

a

b

c

d

e

f

😊 Improve observation skills and attention to detail.

185

Divide the elves into four equal groups.
Colour each group with a different colour.

How many colours did you need?

 Make a start with simple division tasks.

186

Complete the pictures with the missing items.

Write the correct number on each trophy, using the clues to help you.

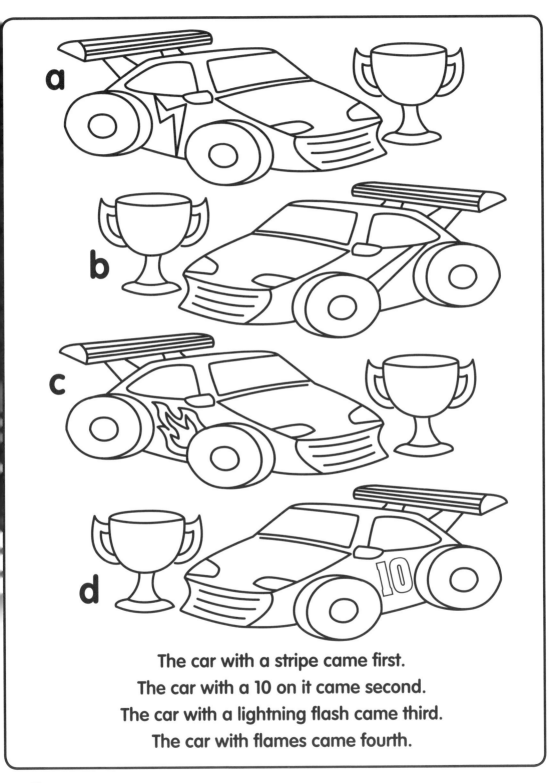

a

b

c

d

The car with a stripe came first.
The car with a 10 on it came second.
The car with a lightning flash came third.
The car with flames came fourth.

 Learn the cardinal numbers: first, second, third and so on.

188

Find two sea monsters that match each other exactly.

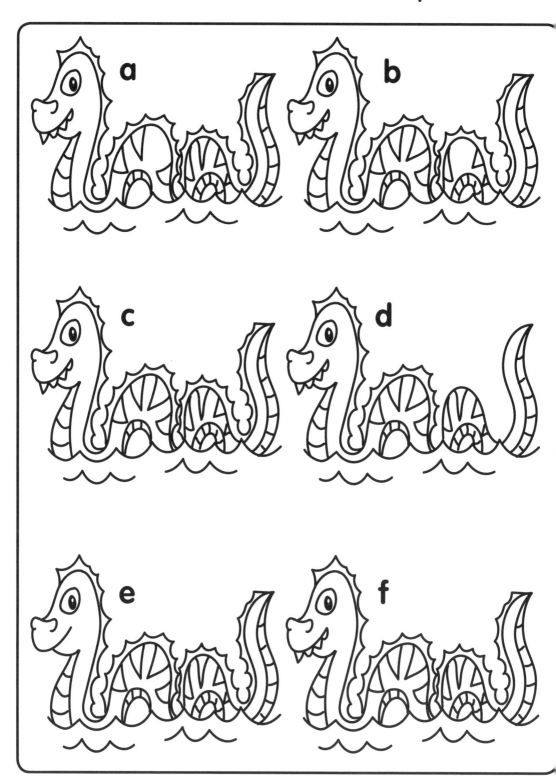

189

Work out the answers using the number line to help you.

6 + 3 =

7 − 4 =

4 + 4 =

8 − 6 =

1   2   3   4   5   6   7   8   9   10

😊 Bounce along the line in both directions!

190 Put the pictures in the right order to tell a story, writing the numbers 1 to 4 in the spaces.

😊 Understand how a story progresses in logical order.

191

Find each of the words hidden in the grid.
What links them all together?

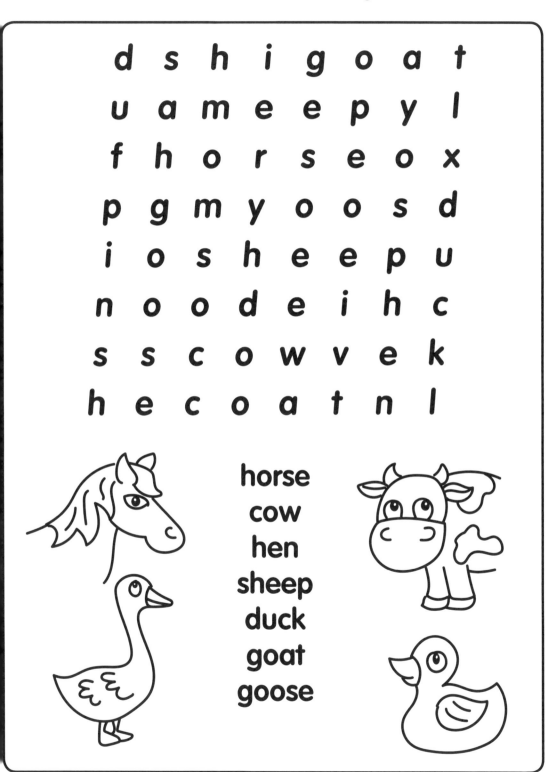

```
d  s  h  i  g  o  a  t
u  a  m  e  e  p  y  l
f  h  o  r  s  e  o  x
p  g  m  y  o  o  s  d
i  o  s  h  e  e  p  u
n  o  o  d  e  i  h  c
s  s  c  o  w  v  e  k
h  e  c  o  a  t  n  l
```

horse
cow
hen
sheep
duck
goat
goose

 Practise spellings and see what words have in common.

192

Do the picture sums and write the answer as a number each time.

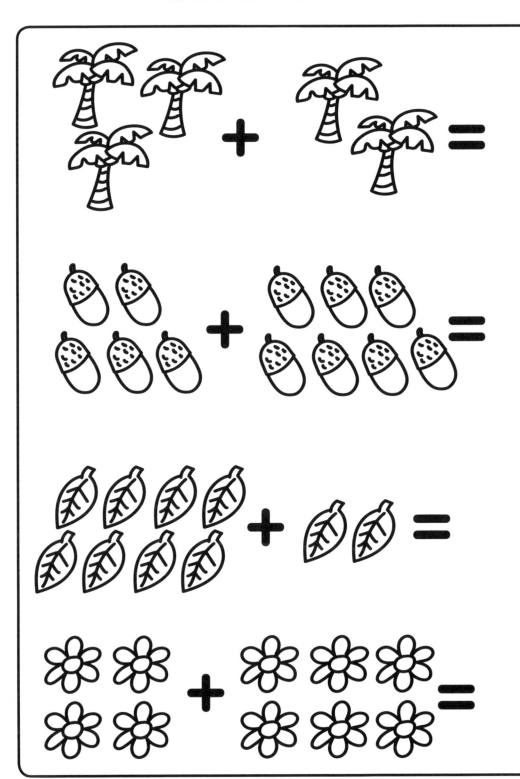

Which of the pesky pirates
is the odd one out?

194

Finish drawing the pattern on each princess's dress.

195

Draw four more spots on his scarf.

Draw two more buttons on his coat.

Draw three more stripes on his shirt.

 Have fun learning about numbers written as words.

196

Find the letters that appear twice and cross them out. The others spell a food.

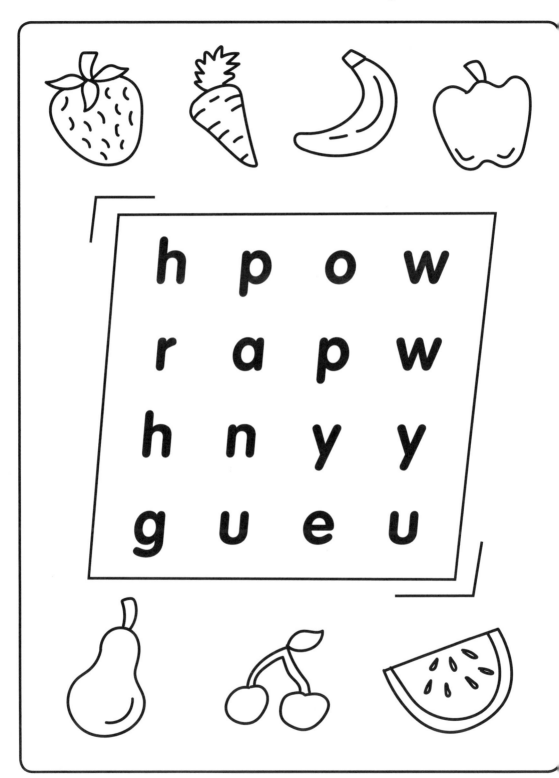

h	p	o	w
r	a	p	w
h	n	y	y
g	u	e	u

Look for familiar letters and practise spelling.

197

**Finish the cakes so each
one has four candles on it.**

198

Colour the picture using the word sounds to guide you.

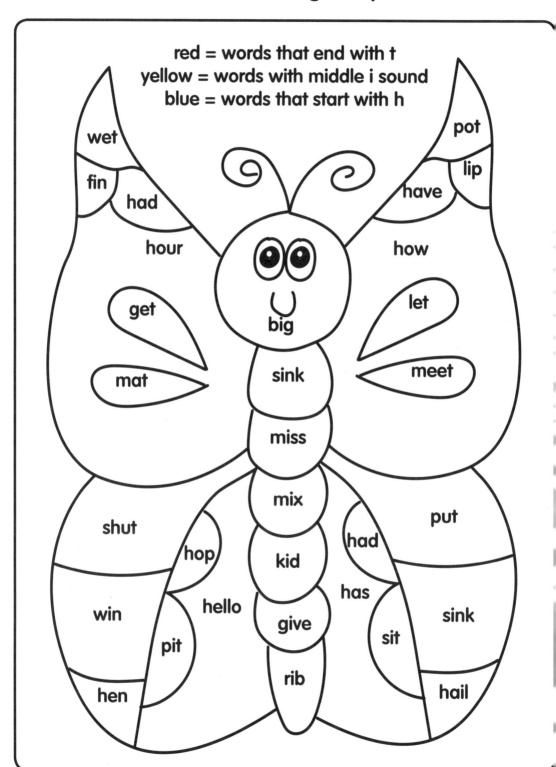

red = words that end with t
yellow = words with middle i sound
blue = words that start with h

wet

pot

fin

lip

had

have

hour

how

get

let

big

mat

sink

meet

miss

mix

shut

put

hop

had

kid

hello

has

win

sink

give

pit

sit

rib

hen

hail

Draw the hands on the clocks to show the important times for Cinderella.

7 o'clock

12 o'clock

200

Join the dots in the correct order to
see what is in the magic mirror.

201 Look at the pattern formed on each line of faces. Fill in the blank circles with the correct face to follow the pattern.

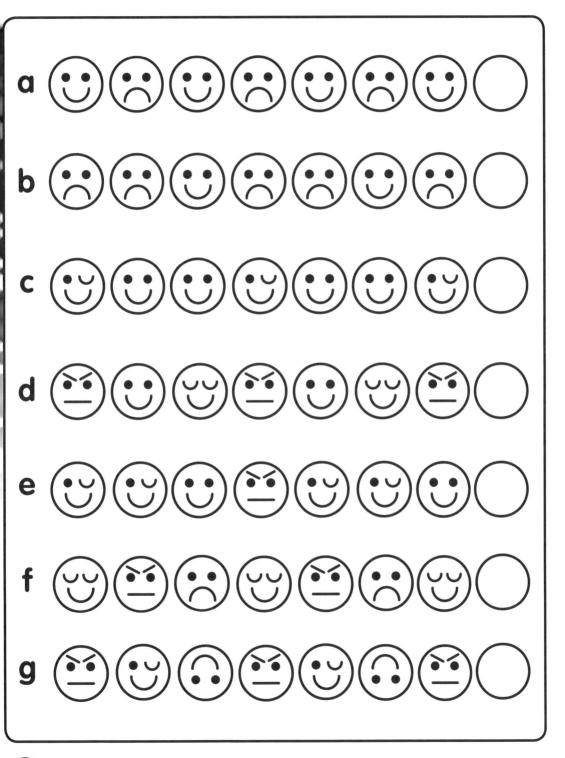

202

Where do the missing pieces fit in the jigsaw?

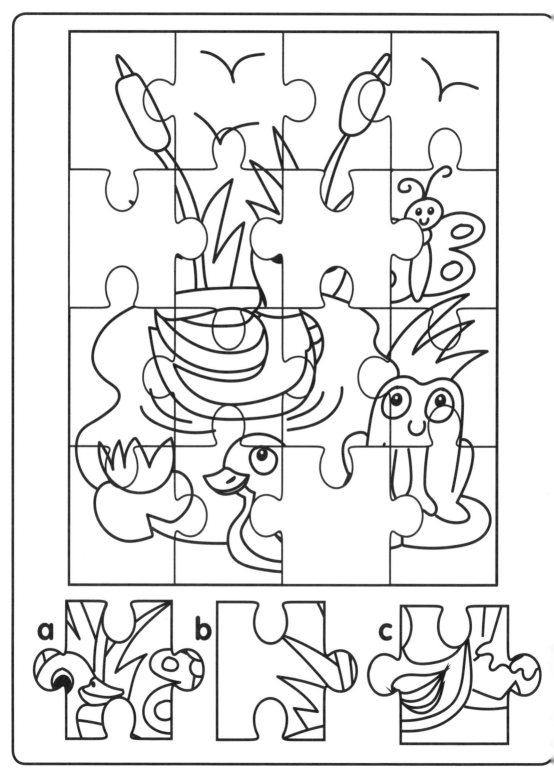

😊 **Study how shapes fit together.**

Use the number ladder to help
you solve these problems.

4 - 2 =

10 - 6 =

8 - 5 =

5 - 3 =

7 - 4 =

1
2
3
4
5
6
7
8
9
10

Number ladders can help with subtraction, too.

**Read the story out loud and
then colour the picture to match.**

Redbeard the pirate yawned and stretched. It was
nearly bedtime. He took off his blue coat with the
golden buttons. He folded his purple trousers and laid
them on top of his brown boots. Arrr! G'night, everyone!

 Have fun with storytelling and description!

Find two toadstools for each fairy
so they add up to 10 each time.

206

Which shape goes in the empty space?

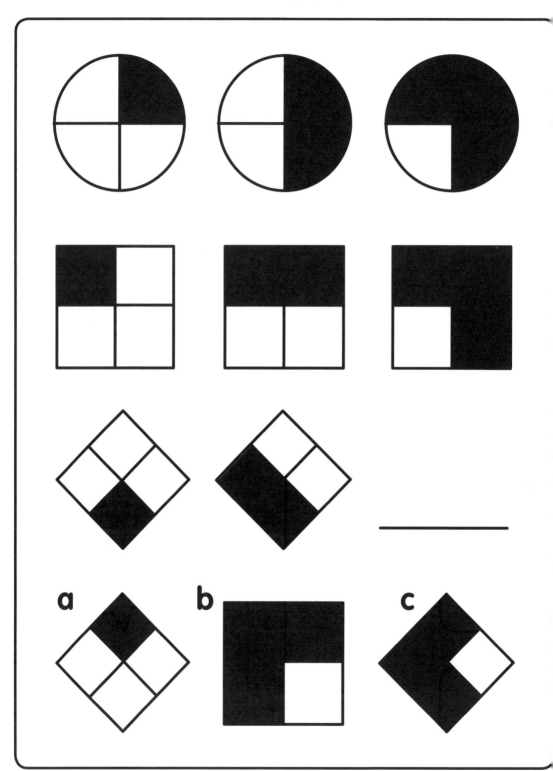

Count up the items in the picture and write totals in the boxes.

Change one letter in each word to make the new word.

cake

_ _ _ _

mole

_ _ _ _

seal

_ _ _ _

lock

_ _ _ _

 Get to grips with simple spelling.

Cross out the double letters and use the leftover letters to spell a fun activity.

o	o	c	a	u
m	p	r	r	u
i	n	q	q	s
g	f	h	f	h
t	t	b	b	s

Improve observation skills and spelling.

What sound does each animal make?
Say them out loud and copy the words.

horse
nay!

_____

mouse
eek!

_____

tiger
roar!

_____

 What other animal noises can you make together?

Find each of the sporting words
hidden in the grid.

```
s  s  e  r  v  e  h  s
w  c  y  c  r  e  o  k
h  y  l  b  u  m  p  s
i  c  s  k  n  a  l  w
t  l  t  h  r  o  w  i
h  e  u  m  p  s  e  m
j  u  m  p  s  k  i  p
t  h  r  a  l  h  e  m
```

jump **throw** **serve**
run   **skip**   **cycle**
swim **hit**

😊 Recognise verbs and learn how to spell them.

Which are there more of, bees or flowers?

☺ **Practise counting and then comparing the numbers.**

**Answer the questions using
the picture to help you.**

Where has Jack climbed to?

How did he get there?

Who has he found at the top?

What might he do next?

🙂 Use context and imagination to answer questions.

Answers

Check here to see which questions were
answered correctly. Add the star stickers
in the special reward spaces.

1. bark, shark
   rain, chain
   pair, chair

2. The middle kitten is
   on its own.

3. There are more
   jewels on her dress
   than on her cloak.
   Dress = 10
   Cloak = 7

4. d

5. Look for two of
   these items: gloves,
   slippers, shoes,
   socks, and tennis
   racquets and balls.

6. hippo – potamus
   kanga – roo
   rhino – ceros
   croc – odile

7. Reward yourself with
   a star for good work.

8. dragon
   wizard
   fairy

9. Give yourself a star
   if you filled in all the
   letters from
   a to z.

10. c and f

11. Stick a star here
    if you had fun
    colouring the
    picture.

12. True
    False
    True
    False

13.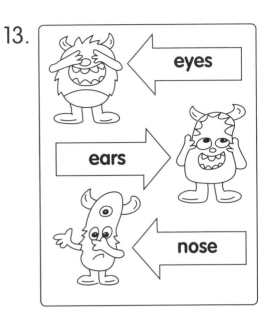

14. Did you spot these
    things?
    wand, wings,
    watermelon, wall,
    window, web, worm

15. a

16. dig, pen, jar

17. Stick a star here if you filled in all the numbers from 1 to 9.

18. fly, swim, run, hop

19. Award yourself a star if you found all six wands.

20. Did you match the words to the pictures? Stick a star here.

21.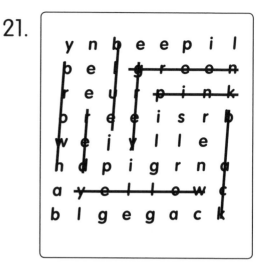

22. 55 =

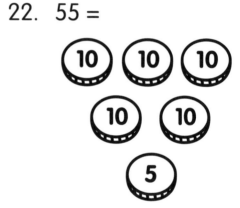

23. nose ear
    arm hand
    foot leg

24.

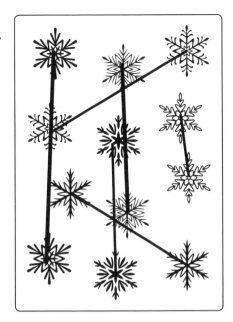

27. Did you join the pairs correctly? Give yourself a star!

28. 3 + 3 = 6

2 + 5 = 7

6 + 2 = 8

7 − 3 = 4

9 − 4 = 5

25. Give yourself a star if you finished the whole alphabet.

29. feet

cake

fish

pond

26. cap = map

cheese = keys

witch = switch

cat = rat

30.

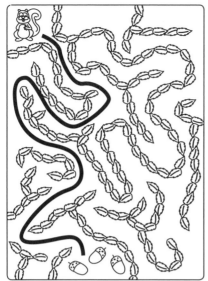

31.

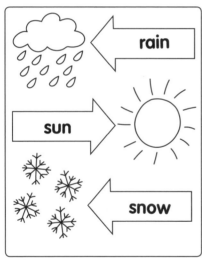

32. Stick a star here if you circled 13 capital letters.

33. pet and vet rhyme

cub, tub and scrub rhyme

six, tricks and sticks rhyme

34. If you think you matched all the words and pictures, give yourself a star.

35.

36.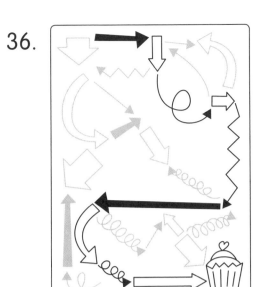

37. If you used 3 colours for three sets of owls, award yourself a star here.

38. i

fish, ring, lips, witch, milk, bridge

39. The plane is above the clouds. The helicopter is below the clouds. The plane looks old. The helicopter looks new.

40. sh

flash, dish, fish, brush, bush

41. You should have filled in f, g, j, l, n, p, r, t, v and x to complete the alphabet.

42. d

43. The –a– sound words are all in triangles.

44. cat – cut
bug – bag
man – men
mop – map

45. d and e

46. Not happy = sad
Not fat = thin
Not light = dark
Not short = tall
Not good = bad

47. d

48. goose
sad
sheep

49. Did you spot these things?
cloud, cactus
cowboy, kettle,
cow, cat,
campfire

50. Give yourself a star if you are happy with your patterns.

51.

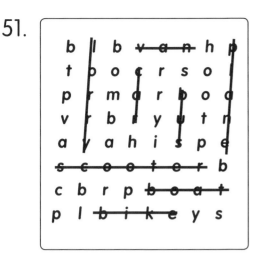

```
b  l  b  v  a  n  h  p
t  p  o  c  r  s  o
p  r  m  a  r  b  o  d
v  r  b  l  y  u  t  n
a  y  a  h  i  s  p  e
s  c  o  o  t  e  r  b
c  b  r  p  b  o  a  t
p  l  b  i  k  e  y  s
```

52. Did you find the fish?

53. These things are out of place: astronaut, rabbit up a tree, saucepan, snake in the girl's hand

54. Award yourself a star if you found lots of circles.

55. Does your owl look beautiful?

56. a = I deliver letters.
b = I look after sick people.
c = I cook delicious food.
d = I mend cars.

57. The food is BANANA.

58. f

59. This is not a sentence:
Puddles floor.
This is not true for the picture: The boy is in the bath.

60. Bang the drum
    and the triangle.
    Blow the recorder
    and the trumpet.

61. s

62. a

63. You should match
    these:
    one = 1
    five = 5
    20 = twenty
    ten = 10
    2 = two

64. Sea: fish, seaweed,
    eel, rock
    Sky: plane, sun,
    moon

65. Stick a star here
    if you tried hard
    to think of your
    answers.

66.

67.

1 o'clock

5 o'clock

68. Did you give each monkey three bananas?
Have a star!

69. Reward yourself with a sticker if you filled in all the blanks.

70. Did you add windows to the house, hands on the watch, petals on the flower, and wheels on the truck? Well done!

71.

start

finish

72. You should have coloured 4 groups of stars.

73. Did you have fun making the noises while you were writing?

74. The foods are pear, pie, pizza, pumpkin, pancakes, pineapple. They all begin with p.

75. Cassie learnt how to bake a cake. Jamie needs some glue for his shoe. It is too hot to run in the sun.

76. 1. Choose a bowl and spoon.
    2. Tip cereal into the bowl.
    3. Pour on the milk.
    4. Put the milk back in the fridge.

77. Give yourself a star if you finished each dragon with six spikes.

78. a = 3
    b = 1
    c = 2

79.

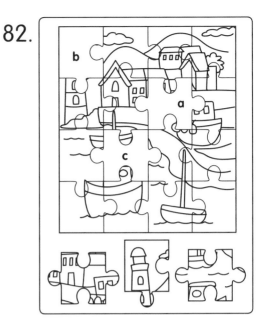

82.

80. True
False
True
False

83. bag
log
shoe

81. Colin = camel
Emily = elephant
Wendy = wolf

84. Cheese a has the
right letters.

85. Monster a

86. Give yourself a star reward if you found all 11 capital letters.

87. The crowns will now have 3, 6, 5 and 4 jewels.

88. The rabbit

89. Not here = there
Not low = high
Not inside = outside
Not dry = wet

90. c and f

91. Bang the cymbals and the xylophone. Blow the saxophone and the trombone.

92. c

93. fly, eye, cry

94. 7 + 2 = 9
5 + 5 = 10
3 + 4 = 7
4 + 5 = 9

95. 10 blocks tall

96. bat, fill, leg

97. $2 + 4 = 6$
    $3 + 3 = 6$
    $6 + 2 = 8$
    $5 + 4 = 9$
    $8 + 1 = 9$

98. 1. Empty your
       things from inside.
    2. Take out the
       tent poles.
    3. Fold the tent
       neatly.
    4. Put the tent in
       its bag.

99. cat – bat – mat – rat
    – flat – hat – bat

100.

101.

b w u b w a n t
e k b e t l e
s m f e c r i o
w u   w f l o
a m e c k e t
s k d m o t h y
e a m o a s p
c r i c k e t l

102. c

103. b

104. These are not seaside words: reindeer, radiator, crown, toothpaste, rocket

105. $4 + 6 = 10$

$7 + 3 = 10$

$2 + 8 = 10$

106. beetle

107. The middle kite has flown the highest.

108. It's time for a star after making all those noises!

109. 5 moons = odd

3 bolts = odd

2 rats = even

6 stars = even

110. Give yourself a star if you found all six arrows.

111. lake – cake

lake – rake

lake – lace

lake – bake

112. 15, 17, 24, 21

113. Your monster should be nice and colourful when you've finished!

114. They can all be found in the kitchen.

115. Here are some ideas:
be: bed, beg, bee
to: toe, top, too
it: lit, hit, sit
no: not, now, nod
we: wet, web, wee
go: got, god, goo

116. I <u>climb</u> up the ladder.
He <u>lies</u> on the rug.
She <u>buys</u> some apples.
The dog <u>barks</u> loudly.

117. You should have 6 yellow lemons and 6 green limes.

118. Tower b is the tallest. Tower c is the smallest.

119. She needs 18 buttons altogether (or 15 more, as she has sewn 3 already).

120. Did you find the group with 7 fish? Stick a star here.

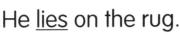

121. Not weak = strong
Not down = up
Not old = young
Not small = big

122.

125. They spell
BEEP BEEP!

126. The balloons belong
to <u>him</u>.
The presents belong
to <u>me</u>.

123. 2 + 3 = 5
4 + 6 = 10
7 + 1 = 8
10 – 5 = 5
3 – 2 = 1

127. 4 + 4 = 8
6 + 8 = 14
2 + 4 = 6
3 + 5 = 8

124. Did you use some
lovely colours? Stick
a star here if you are
pleased with your
work.

128. The unicorn ate
grass for breakfast.

129. 6 + 4 = 10

2 + 9 = 11

7 + 5 = 12

9 − 3 = 6

12 − 6 = 6

14 − 4 = 10

130. You should have coloured 20, 40, 50, 60 and 80.

131.

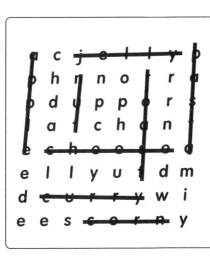

132. White bats

133. Give yourself a star reward if you used all the words correctly.

134. 3

135.

136. The shark

137. What times did
you draw?
Stick a star here.

138. Place a star here
if you are happy
with your writing.

139. 2 + 5 + 7 = 14
8 + 4 + 1 = 13
5 + 3 + 9 = 17
6 + 8 + 2 = 16

140. Great noises!
Well done!

141. You should have 4
green vans and 4
orange ones.

142.

143. 5 jewels = odd
8 hearts = even
11 flowers = odd
2 butterflies = even

144. d

145. Not cold = warm
     Not hard = soft
     Not awake = asleep
     Not short = long

146. You should have a
     total of 15 chicks.

147. Did you find the
     unicorn? Give
     yourself a star.

148. fly, cry
     mouse, house
     star, car

149. These are the odd
     numbers: 1, 3, 5, 7,
     9, 11

150. The clown starts in
     his underwear, adds
     trousers, puts on his
     shirt, and finishes
     with his hat, funny
     shoes, and
     make-up.

151. $9 + 1 + 4 = 14$
     $6 + 4 + 2 = 12$
     $5 + 5 + 6 = 16$

152.

153. Do you deserve a star for filling in your family tree carefully?

154. You should have found Katy's apple, cupcake, drink and sandwich.

155. Add a star here if you coloured the red and blue cars in the mud.

156. hand, flag, toast, plant

157. Use a star sticker to show how well you've done!

158. b and d

159. This is not a sentence: Happy dog. This is not true for this picture: The dog is in front.

160. a

161. Did you spot these things? dungarees, dog, dragonfly, duck You might have said daughter, too?

162. c

163. guitar = hand
tambourine = hand
trumpet = mouth
recorder = mouth

164.

8 o'clock

7 o'clock

165. Did you make each monster happy with five lollipops? Add a star!

166. lip – drip – zip
– pip – skip – ship

167. 40 – 50 – 60 – 70 –
80 – 90 – 100

168. Fill them with more
stripes, spots and
spirals.

169. I

170. a = I can paint
your room.
b = I will cut
your hair.
c = I make
TV shows.
d = I do science
experiments.

171.
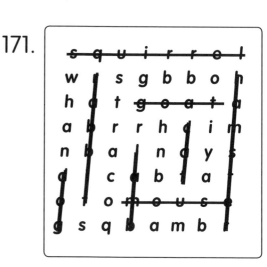

172. $4 + 7 = 11$
$9 + 3 = 12$
$2 + 6 = 8$
$5 + 1 = 6$

173. Did you add all
the wheels? Have
another star!

174. Not early = late
Not short = long
Not quiet = loud
Not standing = lying

175. Stick a sticker here if you drew all the new craters.

176. fish
pen
hand

177. a and d

178. You deserve another star for great writing!

179. The dogs are 10, 8 and 7 blocks long.

180. You should have 6 of each colour.

181. The little <u>monkey</u> couldn't believe it. This was a <u>magic</u> carpet! Up, up, up into the sky he flew, until he felt that he could touch the <u>moon</u>.

182. $6 - 3 = 3$
$8 - 3 = 5$
$4 - 3 = 1$
$7 - 3 = 4$

183. Toadstool 2

184. e

185. You would need 3 colours.

186. Add another star
here if you're happy
with your drawings.

187. a = 3

b = 1

c = 4

d = 2

188. c and f

189. 6 + 3 = 9

7 − 4 = 3

4 + 4 = 8

8 − 6 = 2

190. 1 = d

2 = b

3 = c

4 = a

191.

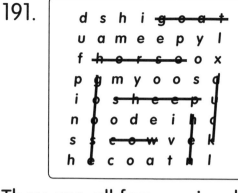

They are all farm animals.

192. 3 + 2 = 5

5 + 7 = 12

8 + 2 = 10

4 + 6 = 10

193. c

194. Place a sticker
here if you finished
decorating the
dresses.

195. Did you follow all the
instructions to dress
the pirate?

196. The food is: orange.

197. Reward yourself with a sticker if each cake has 4 candles now.

198. Does your butterfly look bright and bold now?

199.

200. Did you reveal the wicked queen?

201.

202.

203. 4 − 2 = 2

10 − 6 = 4

8 − 5 = 3

5 − 3 = 2

7 − 4 = 3

204. Are you pleased with your colourful character? Have a star!

205. 9 + 1 = 10

5 + 5 = 10

3 + 7 = 10

206. c

207.

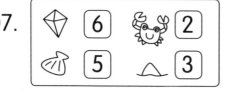

| | 6 | | 2 |
| | 5 | | 3 |

208. cake – cane

mole – hole

seal – meal

lock – sock

209. camping

210. Was it very noisy while you were on that page?!

211.

```
s  c  o  r  v  e  h  s
w  c  y  c  r  e  o  k
h  y  l  b  u  m  p  s
i  d  s  k  n  a  l  w
t  l  t  h  r  o  w  i
h  e  u  m  p  s  e  m
j  u  m  p  s  k  i  p
t  h  r  a  l  h  e  m
```

212. There are more flowers.

213. Did you think of interesting answers? Have a final star sticker for all your hard work!